PIANO • VOCAL • GUITAR

ISBN 0-7935-3523-9

7777 W. BLUEMOUND RD. P.O. BOX 13819 MILWAUKEE, WI 53213

August and Everything After

ANNA BEGINS

Words and Music by ADAM DURITZ, DAVID BRYSON,
MATT MALLEY, STEVE BOWMAN, CHARLIE GILLINGHAM,
MARTIN JONES, TOBY HAWKINS and LYDIA HOLLY

Moderately (not too fast)

GHOST TRAIN

Words and Music by ADAM DURITZ, DAVID BRYSON,
MATT MALLEY, STEVE BOWMAN and CHARLIE GILLINGHAM

I took the can-non-ball _____ down _____ to _____ the o - cean, _____
She buys a tick-et _____ 'cause _____ it's cold where _____ she comes _____ from. _____
_____ to _____ the o - cean, _____

a - cross _____ the des - ert _____ from _____ sea _____ to shin - ing _____ sea.
She climbs a - board _____ be-cause she's scared _____ of get-ting old - er in the snow.
watched _____ the die - sel dis - ap-pear _____ be-neath the tum-bl-ing waves.

MR. JONES

Words and Music by ADAM DURITZ, DAVID BRYSON,
MATT MALLEY, STEVE BOWMAN and CHARLIE GILLINGHAM

Sha - la - la - la - la - la - la.

Uh huh.

I was down at the New Am - ster - dam

18

OMAHA

Words and Music by ADAM DURITZ, DAVID BRYSON,
MATT MALLEY, STEVE BOWMAN and CHARLIE GILLINGHAM

and get your mon-ey back at the door.

PERFECT BLUE BUILDINGS

Words and Music by ADAM DURITZ, DAVID BRYSON, MATT MALLEY, STEVE BOWMAN and CHARLIE GILLINGHAM

D.S. al Coda

A MURDER OF ONE

Words and Music by ADAM DURITZ, DAVID BRYSON,
MATT MALLEY, STEVE BOWMAN and CHARLIE GILLINGHAM

RAIN KING

Words and Music by ADAM DURITZ, DAVID BRYSON,
MATT MALLEY, STEVE BOWMAN and CHARLIE GILLINGHAM

Af - ter all ___ the dream - ing, ___ I ___

__ come home _____ a - gain... ___ *Organ solo*

D.S. al Coda

Solo ends

ROUND HERE

Words and Music by ADAM DURITZ, DAVID BRYSON,
MATT MALLEY, STEVE BOWMAN, CHARLIE GILLINGHAM,
CHRIS ROLDAN, DAN JEWETT and DAVE JANUSCO

<u>*Circles*</u>

running in circles
trying to catch
the essence
of you
but you are already gone
or
were you ever
really there?

Karen Ley

Rest

rest now
here in the earth
the wind plays with me
carries my screams
so i can be heard
a storm lies in wait
i sense it
touch it
feel it
smell it
taste it
the wind calls to me
i follow
it leads me to the rain
i wash my sins
i make them clean
like a slate
i lay in the clouds
the wind whispers
rest now

Karen Ley

RAINING IN BALTIMORE

Words and Music by ADAM DURITZ,
MATT MALLEY and CHARLIE GILLINGHAM

SULLIVAN STREET

Words and Music by ADAM DURITZ, DAVID BRYSON,
MATT MALLEY, STEVE BOWMAN and CHARLIE GILLINGHAM

TIME AND TIME AGAIN

Words and Music by ADAM DURITZ, DAVID BRYSON,
MATT MALLEY, STEVE BOWMAN,
CHARLIE GILLINGHAM and DON DIXON

Moderately slow

no chord

I want-ed so ___ bad - ly ___ some - bod - y oth-er than ___ me ___ star-ing ___ back ___